Crimes and Criminals of the Holocaust

Titles in The Holocaust in History Series

**Crimes and Criminals
of the Holocaust**
0-7660-1995-0

**The Forgotten Victims
of the Holocaust**
0-7660-1993-4

**Hitler's Rise
to Power
and the Holocaust**
0-7660-1991-8

**Impact of
the Holocaust**
0-7660-1996-9

**The Jewish Victims
of the Holocaust**
0-7660-1992-6

**Resisters and Rescuers—
Standing up Against the
Holocaust**
0-7660-1994-2

—The Holocaust in History—

Crimes and Criminals of the Holocaust

Linda Jacobs Altman

 **Enslow Publishers, Inc.**
40 Industrial Road　　　　PO Box 38
Box 398　　　　　　　　　Aldershot
Berkeley Heights, NJ 07922　Hants GU12 6BP
USA　　　　　　　　　　UK
http://www.enslow.com

Purchased with funds from the
Allegheny Regional Asset District

Copyright © 2004 by Linda Jacobs Altman

All rights reserved.

No part of this book may be reproduced by any means without the written permission of the publisher.

Library of Congress Cataloging-in-Publication Data

Altman, Linda Jacobs, 1943–
  Crimes and criminals of the Holocaust / Linda Jacobs Altman.
    p. cm. — (The Holocaust in history)
  Summary: Describes the atrocities committed against Jews, Gypsies, the handicapped, and other minorities in the German concentration camps, and the many trials which brought to justice some of those who were responsible.
  Includes bibliographical references (p.) and index.
  ISBN 0-7660-1995-0
  1. Holocaust, Jewish (1939–1945)—Juvenile literature. 2. War criminals—Germany—Juvenile literature. 3. Nuremberg Trial of Major German War Criminals, Nuremberg, Germany, 1945–1946—Juvenile literature. [1. Holocaust, Jewish (1939–1945) 2. War criminals.] I. Title. II. Series.
  D804.34.A47 2004
  940.53'18—dc22
                                              2003019759

Printed in the United States of America

10 9 8 7 6 5 4 3 2 1

To Our Readers: We have done our best to make sure all Internet Addresses in this book were active and appropriate when we went to press. However, the author and the publisher have no control over and assume no liability for the material available on those Internet sites or on other Web sites they may link to. Any comments or suggestions can be sent by e-mail to comments@enslow.com or to the address on the back cover.

Illustration Credits: Belarrussian State Archive of Documentary Film and Photography, courtesy of USHMM, pp. 11, 15; Courtesy of Simon Wiesenthal Center Library and Archives, Los Angeles, CA, pp. 75, 76, 81, 84, 89; Enslow Publishers, Inc., p. 8; © Evvy Eisen, p. 87; KZ Gedenkstatte Dachau, courtesy of USHMM, p. 66; National Archives and Records Administration, pp. 1, 2, 3, 5, 6, 10, 17, 21, 53; State Archives of the Russian Federation, courtesy of USHMM, p. 67; USHMM, p. 30; USHMM, courtesy of Alex Hochhauser, p. 38; USHMM, courtesy of Alice Lev, pp. 24, 25; USHMM, courtesy of Central Armed Forces Museum, p. 62; USHMM, courtesy of Gerald Schwab, pp. 40, 45, 47; USHMM, courtesy of Harry S Truman Library, pp. 44, 51, 55, 57; USHMM, courtesy of Hedwig Wachenheimer Epstein, p. 65; USHMM, courtesy of Israel Government Press Office, pp. 37, 79; USHMM, courtesy of John W. Mosenthal, p. 41; USHMM, courtesy of Lilo Plaschkes, p. 27; USHMM, courtesy of Main Commission for the Prosecution of the Crimes Against the Polish Nation, pp. 60, 72; USHMM, courtesy of Murray T. Aronoff, p. 36; USHMM, courtesy of National Archives and Records Administration, pp. 12, 14, 48, 59, 63, 68, 70.

Cover Illustration: Courtesy of Simon Wiesenthal Center Library and Archives, Los Angeles, C.A. (right); USHMM, Courtesy of Harry S Truman Library (left).

Contents

Introduction: World War II
and the Holocaust 7

1 A Time of Reckoning 11

2 The Victims 24

3 The Nuremberg Trials 40

4 "I Was Just Doing My Job" 59

5 Fugitives From Justice 75

Timeline 91

Chapter Notes 94

Glossary 98

Further Reading 101

Internet Addresses 102

Index 103

On November 9, 1935, thousands of Nazi troops assembled for roll call in Nuremberg, Germany.

Introduction
World War II and the Holocaust

On September 1, 1939, German troops invaded Poland. Two days later, Britain and France declared war on Germany. World War II had begun. Under Adolf Hitler and his National Socialist German Workers' party, also called the Nazi party, Germany would soon conquer most of Europe.

Hitler planned to build a *Reich*, or empire, that would last for a thousand years. He believed that Northern Europeans, or Aryans as he called them, were a master race—a group of people superior to others.

Hitler falsely believed that some people, such as Jews, homosexuals, Gypsies, Poles, Russians, and people of color, were inferior. These people would be given no rights in his Reich. Some would be exterminated, or killed. Others would be kept alive only so long as they served their Aryan masters. It was a dark and terrible vision that cost millions of lives.

In the early days of the war, Germany seemed unbeatable. One nation after another fell to the German *blitzkrieg*, or "lightning war." The Nazis conquered Poland in just twenty-six days. Denmark, Norway, Belgium, the Netherlands, and France fell in the spring of 1940.

By the end of 1940, the Germans had occupied most of Western Europe and made alliances with Italy and Japan. The Axis, as this alliance was called, soon conquered

By the end of 1940, the German army had occupied most of Western Europe, including Poland, Austria, Denmark, Norway, France, Belgium, and the Netherlands.

Introduction: World War II and the Holocaust

parts of Asia, Eastern Europe, and North Africa.

In 1941, the picture changed. In June, Germany invaded the Soviet Union, now called Russia. America entered the war on December 7, after Japan attacked the U.S. naval base in Pearl Harbor, Hawaii. The Germans soon found themselves fighting the British and the Americans in the West, and the Soviets in the East. They also devoted men and resources to exterminating Jews and other people the Nazis saw as inferior.

Even when the war turned against Germany, this slaughter did not stop. Trains that could have carried troops and supplies to the fighting fronts were used instead to transport victims to death camps. The killing continued until the last possible moment.

After Germany surrendered on May 7, 1945, survivors began telling what they had suffered. Pictures of starving prisoners, mass graves, and gas chambers disguised as showers appeared in newspapers and movie newsreels. People all over the world were horrified.

As survivors told their stories, the horror grew. New words came into the language. Old words took on new meanings. *Holocaust* came to represent mass murder on a scale that had never been seen before. *Genocide*

Crimes and Criminals of the Holocaust

On December 19, 1938, prisoners of the Sachsenhausen concentration camp in Germany somberly walk in two lines past their Nazi guards.

described the systematic killing of specific racial or ethnic groups.

These words are reminders of a grim truth—human beings can do terrible things to one another. This is why knowledge about the Holocaust is so important. It is the best defense against the hatred that produced the Nazi racist state and caused the death of innocent millions.

1

A Time of Reckoning

Adolf Hitler wanted to create a Reich, an empire that would last a thousand years. It lasted twelve. In that time, Germany laid waste to much of Europe. Cities crumbled. As many as 50 million people died. At least 11 million were not casualties of war in the usual sense. They were casualties of hatred.

German leaders knew that they would have to pay for these civilian deaths. The prospect frightened many of them. As the war turned against Germany, they tried to cover their tracks.

The Principle of Accountability

The Nazi leaders were right to be worried about their fate after an Allied victory. Even before the full horror of the death camps was

Crimes and Criminals of the Holocaust

known, terrible news came out of German-occupied territory: mass executions, slave labor camps, brutality in many different forms.

In 1944, Henry Morgenthau, Jr., secretary of the treasury in President Franklin D. Roosevelt's Cabinet, called for immediate execution of the chief Nazi leaders. These "arch-criminals," as he called the Nazis, would be arrested, identified, and "executed

Henry Morgenthau, Jr., was the highest ranking Jewish member of President Franklin D. Roosevelt's administration. A report he wrote to Roosevelt led to the creation of the War Refugee Board.

[immediately] by firing squads made up of soldiers of the United Nations."[1]

Secretary of War Henry L. Stimson countered the Morgenthau plan with one of his own. He wanted to place accused criminals on trial before a court. This would establish guilt on an individual basis. It would also provide a complete and permanent record of Nazi crimes.

Neither Stimson nor anyone else recommended leniency, generosity, or forgiveness. Punishment for the guilty should be severe. If ever there was doubt of this, it vanished when the concentration camp liberations began.

The Soviet army, fighting its way through Poland, was first to see the camps. On January 27, 1945, the Soviets liberated Auschwitz. Years after the war, commanding General Vassily Petrenko remembered warehouses filled with the possessions of murdered Jews.

He especially remembered "enormous bundles of women's hair," which the Nazis had planned to use for stuffing mattresses:

> At first I didn't realise [sic] what it was, then somebody told me. . . . The hair of women killed by the Germans and I asked, "How many women do you have to murder to get that much hair?" It's a horrible thing even to think about and a terrible thing to see.[2]

Piles of women's hair were found in a warehouse at the Auschwitz concentration camp.

As other camp liberations followed, Allied anger grew. The Americans, British, and Soviets debated the form of punishment for those responsible. All agreed on one thing: For such horrors, someone had to be held accountable. Even while war still raged in Europe, Allied leaders were laying the foundation for an international tribunal of justice.

The Circle Closes

By the time the Soviets liberated Auschwitz, other parts of the Soviet army had already crossed into Germany. The British and

A Time of Reckoning

Prisoners of Auschwitz celebrate their liberation in January 1945.

Americans were closing in from the west. During the last months of the war, Allied planes bombed German cities into rubble. The Luftwaffe, the German air force, could no longer protect the skies.

Regardless of how bad conditions became on the fighting front, Hitler's orders were the same: Hold ground at all costs. There would be no retreat.

Any German commander who did not hold his position would be dismissed. When General Friedrich Hofsbach fell back from a hopeless position to keep his army from being encircled, Hitler threatened to charge him with treason. The fact that Hofsbach had saved his troops did not matter to Hitler.

Chief of the German General Staff Heinz Guderian tried to sway Hitler with numbers. He pointed out that four hundred thousand German troops were fighting more than 2 million Russians on the eastern front. The Russians had seven tanks for every German tank.

Hitler was not impressed. "The Eastern Front must help itself and make do with what it's got," he told Guderian.[3]

The western front was also collapsing. In March 1945, the British and Americans, along with Canadian and French divisions, crossed the Rhine River into the heart of Germany.

Squadrons of Allied bombers attacked from the air. They struck at everything from fuel depots to cities, laying waste the German heartland. Between January 1945 and the end of the war in May, the Allies dropped 471,000 tons of bombs on Germany.

Many Nazi leaders wanted to sound out the Allies about terms of surrender. Hitler would not hear of it. If Germany was going down, it would go down fighting, he said.

Many Germans saw no reason to continue fighting a war that was obviously lost. Soldiers in the field feared they would never

A Time of Reckoning

An American bomber returns to its base after completing a bombing mission. The target was the Fock Wulf plant in Marienburg, Germany.

see their homes again. One young soldier expressed these feelings in his diary:

> I've now finally given up hope that the war will be won. What an enormous guilt Hitler bears. If I can't see my family again, I don't want to live any longer. Above all, a quick death would be better for them [his family] than to be deported or otherwise tortured.[4]

The Scorched-Earth Policy

Winning the war was everything to Adolf Hitler. He felt that a victory would prove his belief in a German master race. Most of all, it would give him the absolute power he craved. Long after others had realized the war was lost, he tried to convince himself it could still be won.

He ranted and raved. He refused to listen to negative reports. Faith in the Reich was an act of will, he said. He expected his closest associates to cling to that faith: "If you would believe that the war can still be won, if you could at least have faith in that, all would be well. . . . One must believe that all will turn out well."[5]

Those words were spoken in an underground shelter called the Führer bunker. It was topped by an eight-foot thick ceiling, and surrounded by six-foot thick walls. Hitler and his personal staff moved there in January 1945, to escape the constant bombing.

From this hideaway, Hitler continued to run the war. No matter what the situation, his orders were always the same: Never retreat, never surrender. Any soldier who broke and ran should be shot for desertion.

A few of Hitler's associates tried to make him see reason. One of these was Albert Speer, minister of armaments and war production. On March 15, 1945, he wrote Hitler a letter, saying in so many words that the war was lost.

Speer hoped to convince the Führer to stop the fighting and save what could be saved. Hitler's response shocked him: "If the war is lost, then the nation will also perish."[6] He believed that if the German people were not stronger than their enemies, then they did not deserve to survive.

On March 19, Hitler issued an order to destroy everything: power plants, waterworks, ports, factories, communications facilities, roads, and highways. Speer was horrified. He went to work immediately to keep this order from being obeyed.

The Battle for Berlin

On April 16, 1945, at exactly 4 A.M., Soviet artillery opened fire from across the Oder River, thirty-eight miles east of Berlin. As the barrage began, the Soviets turned on 140 large searchlights. One Russian described it as being like "a thousand suns joined together."[7] The last battle of the war in Europe had begun.

Two hours later, another barrage opened to the south, on the Niesse River. Soldiers and equipment began crossing the rivers under cover of the artillery fire.

Though the Soviet bombardment was still thirty-five miles from Berlin, the city's residents could hear the guns thundering in the distance. The thunder moved steadily closer. By April 22, the Russians had cracked the city's southern defenses. Berliners stockpiled food and hid in bomb shelters and basements. Under nearly constant shelling, the city burned.

By this time, Berlin was defended mostly by untrained units of "home guardsmen" and Hitler Youth. The latter was an organization designed to teach German children and teens Nazi beliefs. Hitler expected these older men and teenage boys to stand against the might of the Soviet army. Most of them had only hunting rifles or pistols. Some had no guns at all.

In the streets, people waited numbly for the end. In the Führer bunker, Hitler ordered attacks by units that no longer existed. He continued to tell anyone who would listen that Berlin could yet be saved if only its people had the will.

Hitler's Final Days

Through all his useless planning and talk about will, Hitler never canceled his "scorched earth" orders. Others did it in spite of him. Albert Speer contacted people endlessly,

A Time of Reckoning

Despite grim reports from his generals, Adolf Hitler (standing on left, saluting), refused to accept the defeat of Germany.

begging them not to carry out the order. Others decided on their own that it made no sense.

One chemical plant director called his staff together and read a detailed order for the destruction of all equipment. "Now gentlemen, you know what you are *not* supposed to do," he said.[8] With that, he told the staff good-bye and closed down the plant. Nothing was destroyed.

As the Russians overran Berlin, Hitler could no longer pretend there was any hope. On April 29, he married his longtime girlfriend, Eva Braun. Then he wrote what he called his "political testament." Mostly, it was a rehash of old propaganda slogans. But he could not resist trying to leave a legacy of hatred to future generations: "Above all, I [call upon] the leaders of the nation and those under them to . . . [follow] the laws of race and to [oppose] the universal poisoner of all peoples, International Jewry."[9]

On the morning of April 30, Adolf Hitler and his new wife committed suicide in the Führer bunker. Staff members burned the bodies.

Berlin surrendered to the Russians on May 2. Germany itself surrendered on May 7, 1945. May 8 was declared VE, or "Victory Europe," day. The war in Europe was over.

The Occupation

Victorious Allied troops occupied Germany and its former territories. They faced a huge task. They had to arrest and imprison leading Nazis, help concentration-camp survivors, and form a new government in Germany.

While the occupiers dealt with these problems, diplomats from fifty different nations met in San Francisco. Their chief purpose was to found the United Nations.

They also dealt with Nazi war crimes. They decided that organizations as well as individuals should be held accountable. Some Nazi organizations were by their nature criminal.

For example, the Gestapo were political police, whose job was to ensure public loyalty to Nazism. The Gestapo could arrest and question anyone. Working through a system of spies and informers, the Gestapo became the terror of Germany. Even loyal Nazis feared running afoul of its power. If the organization itself was declared criminal, then every member was guilty of a crime simply by belonging to it.

The United Nations Charter was approved on June 26, 1945, and went into effect on October 24. Nazi Germany had already taught the world one thing: There had to be some form of international justice to prevent such things from happening again.

The Victims

Concentration-camp liberations began long before the end of the war. One of the first camps to be liberated was Majdanek, near Lubin, Poland. The Soviets arrived in July 1944. They found warehouses of poison gas containers, a gas chamber for mass killing, and rows of stone ovens for burning bodies. They also found hundreds of starving, half-dead prisoners who needed immediate care.

That was the way of liberations everywhere. Every camp had its unspeakable horrors, its hundreds or thousands of victims needing help. Every camp had its special tragedies, too—hundreds of prisoners who were simply too far gone to save. Many died within days of liberation.

The Victims

The Displaced Persons Camps

Many refugees ended up in displaced persons (DP), or refugee, camps. They had nowhere else to go. After the Allies divided Germany into four occupation zones (American, British, Soviet, and French), each army became responsible for the DPs in its own area.

Simply finding places to house all these people was a challenge. The Allies used everything from abandoned army bases and prisoner-of-war camps to schoolhouses,

A group of refugees, having just arrived at the Zeilsheim DP camp in Germany, pose for a group portrait.

barns, and even castles. For a time, there was no choice but to keep some people in the same camps where they had been prisoners.

Even those who were moved to different quarters often had to contend with an atmosphere that brought back painful memories. Jacob Biber recalled arriving at Camp Föhrenwald, a DP facility operated by the United Nations Relief and Rehabilitation Administration (UNRRA). He was in a truck with nine other survivors and two soldiers:

> "This is Camp Föhrenwald," shouted Abraham, one of our two escorting soldiers. I had thought that this might be a place of quick transit, a chance [to recover] our energies and spirits, but the word "camp" started my heart pounding in fear again.[1]

Föhrenwald was hardly sinister, but neither was it cheerful. The stunned DPs were ordered to get down from the truck and line up in front of a long brick building. For them, this familiar regimentation was frightening. It became more frightening as others arrived:

> Within minutes the line started to grow. More trucks came through the gates. Passengers [got off] and joined the line. Some of the newcomers, emaciated and pale survivors from the camps, wore thin, black-and-white striped clothing. From other trucks, children of different ages jumped down. These were survivors from all over Europe. The registration line got longer and noisier.[2]

The Victims

UNRRA workers help bathe children at the Kloster Indersdorf DP children's center in Germany.

Föhrenwald was far from the worst of the DP centers. Living conditions at some of them were truly terrible. In part, this was because of problems in organization and supply. The people running these camps were not prepared to handle the problems of ex-prisoners. Many survivors could no longer relate normally to the world.

For example, United Nations relief worker Francesca Wilson recalled children who

> described with complete indifference their blood-curdling experiences—even the murder of their parents—but would storm over some [unimportant] incident: having to wait a week

before having their hair cut again, or a Red Cross parcel without a pot of honey in it. It was clear that their rehabilitation would be difficult.[3]

Even everyday hygiene was a problem. As one American officer observed:

> Even after concentration camp life it is not too much to expect people to flush toilets that are in working order. . . . When a garbage can is provided, is it reasonable to expect them to put the garbage into the can and not on the floor next to the can?[4]

Some officials reacted by continuing to treat displaced persons as prisoners. American general George S. Patton ordered that all DP camps in his zone be surrounded by barbed wire and patrolled by armed guards. This order was cancelled by General Dwight D. Eisenhower, the Allied commander.[5]

The Harrison Report

Eisenhower's order grew out of a report on the terrible conditions in DP camps. In September 1945, a special commission headed by Earl G. Harrison, a law-school dean, inspected camps in the American zone.

Harrison's report to President Harry S Truman was not good:

> . . . we appear to be treating the Jews as the Nazis treated them except that we do not exterminate them. They are in concentration camps . . . under our military guard instead of SS

The Victims

troops. One is led to wonder [if] the German people [suppose] that we are following or at least [accepting] Nazi policy.[6]

There were thousands of incidents and examples Harrison could have reported. At the Rentzschmule DP center, an ex-Nazi was placed in charge of the Jewish DPs. He ignored their needs. A small group of DPs walked sixteen miles to the nearest army base to protest about him.

A Jewish concentration camp survivor, Simon Wiesenthal, was beaten up when he asked for a pass to leave the DP camp of Mauthausen. The man in charge of issuing passes was a Polish ex-prisoner. Wiesenthal recalled that:

> Slowly, slowly I crossed the few yards to [his] office and knocked on the door. He was well nourished compared to us [Jews]. . . . When I asked him for a pass, he [said] that I would have been dead if the Nazis had still been there. Then he beat me up and threw me out into the courtyard.[7]

The Harrison report indirectly put a stop to such abuses, at least in the American zone. After reading it, President Harry S Truman instructed General Eisenhower to order immediate improvements in camp conditions. In addition, the United States government recognized the Jews as "a separate national

Crimes and Criminals of the Holocaust

Earl Harrison's report exposed abuses in the DP camps.

The Victims

category."[8] They could therefore be placed in camps of their own.

Until then, Jews and non-Jews were grouped together by their nation of origin. The new arrangement recognized that Jewish DPs faced special problems.

For Gentile (non-Jewish) ex-prisoners, DP camps were way stations. Before long, most of them would go home. For many Jews, that was impossible. The homes they knew were gone, their property had been seized, and their families were dead. Many of them might spend years as DPs.

Survivor Isabella Leitner wrote about the Jewish plight in her book *Saving the Fragments: From Auschwitz to New York*:

> Those who are returning to their homes and families seem [to understand] . . . that . . . Jewish survivors are a breed separate and apart. No one will be brewing coffee, serving drinks, baking bread and cookies for us at the end of our journey, wherever that end will be. Families will not be waiting for us; no one will be sitting around listening to our war stories. . . . Wherever we go, we will be alien orphans. Home is nowhere for us—not our native land, not in any new land that will have us. We will have to learn a new language, a new culture, a new mode of dress and behavior. We will have to learn to control the rage inside us or make peace with it.[9]

Learning to Live Again

In their own DP camps, Jews of many nations struggled to put their lives back together. It was not an easy task. It meant dealing with enormous physical and psychological damage and deciding how to build new lives. It also meant learning to live with the ghosts of a past that would haunt them the rest of their days.

As people regained their strength, Jewish culture flowered in the camps. In addition to the UNRRA, organizations such as the American Jewish Joint Distribution Committee (also called "the Joint") worked in the camps. They set up schools for the children and job training programs for the adults.

The DPs themselves elected representatives to deal with the camp administration. They published newspapers and formed discussion groups. They held religious services. Some camps even had theater groups.

A big part of the return to life was beginning new families. In some of the larger camps, having ten to twenty weddings per day was common. Most of these newlyweds began having children as quickly as possible.

Family plays an important role in Jewish tradition. Building new families was a way of affirming life in the face of so much death.

The Victims

For most Holocaust survivors, the next step on the road to a normal life was finding a home. That proved to be one of the hardest tasks of all.

The Search for a Home

Many countries—including the United States—were afraid of being swamped with Holocaust refugees. They kept their immigration policies tight. In trying to deal with the needs of the Jewish DPs, the Harrison report recommended that one hundred thousand Jews be allowed to go immediately to Palestine, ancient homeland of the Jewish people.

Helping Jews make a new life in Palestine seemed like a good solution to a difficult problem. There was already an active Jewish community there. Jews had fled massacres in Russia at the turn of the twentieth century. Others came from many different countries during the 1920s and 1930s. They called themselves *Zionists*. Their purpose was to form a new Jewish state in the "land of Zion," another name for Palestine.

The aftermath of the Holocaust gave new urgency to the Zionist goal. Jews in Palestine and around the world believed it was the best solution to the Jewish DP problem.

Unfortunately, the British, who had governed Palestine since World War I, did not agree.

There had already been fighting between Arabs and Jews in the region. Allowing a flood of Jewish immigration could lead to outright war. The British were simply not prepared to risk that. They would allow only a trickle of Jewish immigration.

Not even President Truman could change that. On August 31, 1945, he wrote to the newly elected British prime minister, Clement Attlee: "The main solution appears to lie in the quick evacuation of as many as possible of the [homeless] Jews, who wish it, to Palestine."[10]

Attlee turned down the request:

> In the case of Palestine, we have the Arabs to consider as well as the Jews, and there have been solemn [promises] . . . that before we come to a final decision . . . there would be [discussion] with the Arabs. It would be very unwise to break those solemn pledges and so set aflame the whole Middle East.[11]

Illegal Immigration

The Jews of the Yishuv, as the Jewish community in Palestine was called, did not accept Attlee's decision. They organized illegal immigration to bring Jewish Holocaust survivors to Palestine.

The Victims

From 1945 to the creation of the Jewish state of Israel in 1948, about seventy thousand Jews set out for Palestine. They traveled a long and difficult route, made more hazardous by the need for secrecy. They traveled cross-country, often on foot, to ports on the Mediterranean Sea. From there, they sailed to Palestine, often on run-down, barely seaworthy boats.

More than fifty thousand of the refugees did not make it. Their vessels were caught by the British navy that had blockaded the country. The British sent captured refugees to DP centers to await a solution to the problem of Palestine.

Altogether, some one hundred forty ships attempted to make the crossing. The best known of them was a rickety Chesapeake Bay ferryboat renamed *Exodus 1947*. It sailed from France on July 11, 1947, with some forty five hundred Jewish refugees aboard.

The voyage of the *Exodus* began and ended in full view of the public. At the time, the United Nations was debating the formation of a Jewish state in Palestine. The Jewish-Americans who outfitted and sailed the *Exodus* wanted to dramatize the need for a homeland.

British handling of the crisis helped turn the tide of public opinion in favor of the Jews. In Haifa Harbor in Palestine, British

Crimes and Criminals of the Holocaust

A British boarding party from the H.M.S. *Ajax* heads toward the *Exodus*.

sailors boarded the *Exodus*. When the passengers resisted, the sailors opened fire. Three Jews were killed in the conflict, and dozens were wounded.

After this had raised an outcry, the British decided to "make an example" of the *Exodus*. Instead of placing the refugees in a nearby DP camp, they took them all the way back to Germany.

The plight of these Holocaust survivors moved the world. It also influenced the debate in the United Nations. On November 29, 1947, the UN General Assembly voted to

The Victims

Under the careful eyes of British guards, passengers of the *Exodus* leave their battered ship at the Palestinian port of Haifa.

partition Palestine into two states, one Arab and one Jewish. The state of Israel came into being on May 14, 1948, with the formal end of British rule.

The creation of Israel did not magically empty the DP camps of Europe. Between 1947 and 1950, only half the Jewish DPs remaining in Europe—about one hundred twenty thousand—went to Israel.

Others were not ready for the hardships of life in a pioneering land. They followed earlier emigrants to countries such as the United States, Canada, Australia, and Argentina.

Thousands of people celebrate the founding of the state of Israel outside the headquarters of the Central Committee of the Liberated Jews in Munich, Germany.

Föhrenwald, the last DP camp in Europe, finally closed in February 1957.

It was the end of an era that had lasted nearly a decade. Survivors and many others were not sorry to see it go. Now, the victims of the Holocaust wanted to see their former Nazi captors face justice.

The Nuremberg Trials

With the war over and Europe in shambles, the Allies faced war crimes on a scale never seen before. Putting the criminals on trial was a major goal. Arrests began immediately.

In Berlin, the Soviets soon learned that Adolf Hitler had committed suicide. So had his minister of propaganda, Joseph Goebbels. SS leader Heinrich Himmler had tried to escape. However, he was caught, and he later killed himself in captivity.

The Accused

On October 18, 1945, twenty-four Nazi leaders were indicted, or charged, with crimes. Three of those men would never stand trial. Robert Ley killed himself; Gustav Krupp was

The Nuremberg Trials

too ill to stand trial. Hitler's private secretary, Martin Bormann, was tried *in absentia* (in his absence), because he was never captured.

The twenty-one prisoners who would stand trial represented a cross-section of power in the Reich. There were high government officials, military men, diplomats, economists, propagandists, and high-level administrators.

Hermann Göring and Rudolf Hess were the highest-ranking defendants. For a time, Göring had been the number two man in

The defendants sit and listen during the International Military Tribunal trial for war criminals at Nuremberg.

Germany, after only Hitler himself. Hess was next in line. Although Hitler had turned on both these men and stripped them of power, they would not renounce Nazism.

The highest-ranking military officer was Field Marshal Wilhelm Keitel, chief of the Armed Forces High Command. His defense was his soldier's oath of loyalty to the Führer. He would also point out the impossibility of disobeying Hitler's orders.

The trial of these defendants would be a historic occasion: the first time leaders of any nation had been held accountable before a court of international law. The Palace of Justice in Nuremberg, Germany, was hastily rebuilt for the proceedings.

The Indictments

The defendants were charged with four counts, or types, of crimes: conspiracy, crimes against peace, war crimes, and crimes against humanity.

- *Conspiracy* meant that the Nazis worked together to plan and carry out criminal aggression, or violent acts, against other peoples.
- *Crimes against peace* referred to the actual waging of war and the violation of treaties.
- *War crimes* were criminal actions during the war itself. They included killing civilian

hostages and prisoners of war. They also included destroying whole towns and cities "without military justification or necessity," in the words of the indictment.[1]

- *Crimes against humanity* covered persecution on "political, racial, and religious grounds."[2] It cited the mass murder of Jews and others before and during the war.

The Court

The court convened, or assembled, at the Palace of Justice in Nuremberg. Eight judges sat on the tribunal. There was a chief judge and an alternate from each of four nations: Britain, the United States, the Soviet Union, and France.

Sir Geoffrey Lawrence of Britain was elected president of the court. He kept order in the court and saw to it that the trial ran smoothly.

He also had to deal with disagreements among the judges. With men from different nations, with different political systems and laws, that was a big job. Lawrence proved himself equal to the task. Observers said he had a gift for working out compromises.

Each of the four countries also sent a team of prosecutors. They divided the work so that each nation handled a different crime. This

Crimes and Criminals of the Holocaust

The International Military Tribunal trial of war criminals was held at the Palace of Justice in Nuremberg, Germany.

Sir Geoffrey Lawrence (foreground) takes notes during the trial at Nuremberg.

served the ends of justice and also made the trials more efficient.

The Prosecution

The first public session of the Nuremberg trial began on November 20, 1945. The next day, United States Supreme Court Justice Robert H. Jackson gave the opening address. He did not speak as a justice of the Supreme Court, but as lead prosecutor for the United States:

"The privilege of opening the first trial in history for crimes against the peace of the world imposes a grave responsibility," he said. ". . . We must never forget that the record on which we judge these defendants today is the record on which history will judge us tomorrow."[3]

Everyone who was part of the trial had one eye on history. The court knew it would be creating a permanent record of what the Nazis had done. The fate of twenty-one defendants rested on that record. By exposing Nazi crimes, Nuremberg would send a message to future generations. Even in war, some things would not be tolerated: brutal invasion, senseless destruction, and mass murder on a scale never seen before.

To send this message, the evidence against the defendants had to be compelling. The trial had to be strictly fair. Anything less would seem like victor's justice and taint the verdicts.

Each defendant had a lawyer of his own choosing. He had the right to call witnesses on his behalf and cross-examine, or question, witnesses testifying against him. As Robert Jackson put it, "If these men are the first war leaders of a defeated nation to be prosecuted in the name of the law, they are also the first to be given a chance to plead for their lives in the name of the law."[4]

The Nuremberg Trials

Robert Jackson delivers the opening speech for the American prosecution at the International Military Tribunal trial.

Crimes and Criminals of the Holocaust

To build an airtight case, the prosecution used many documents: books, official papers, memos, letters, diaries, photographs, and films. Said Jackson, "There is no count in the indictment that cannot be proved by books and records. . . . We will show you their own films. You will see their own conduct and hear their own voices. . . ."[5]

This approach kept the prosecution's case focused on recorded fact. However, it did have one flaw—the endless reading of documents into evidence made the proceedings impersonal. Some of the documents were lengthy, others too technical. Many were boring. It was not always easy to remember that behind the facts and figures were real people. Some of those people did terrible things.

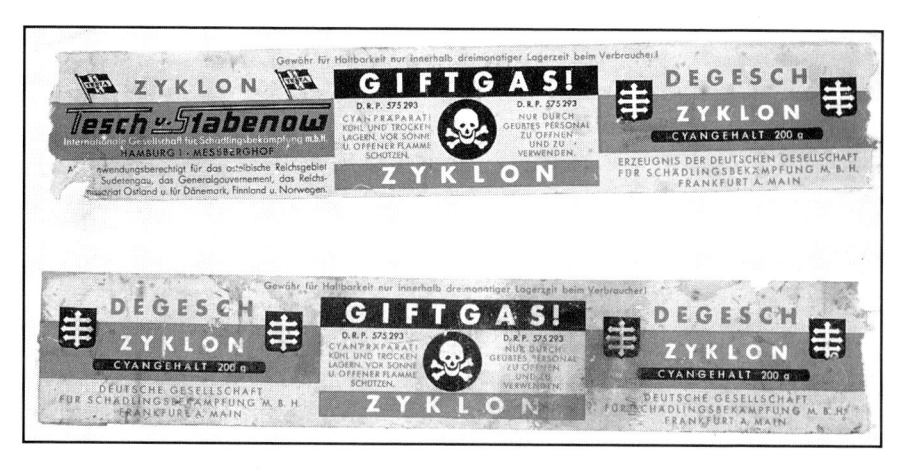

These labels from Zyklon B canisters were used as evidence during the Nuremberg trial. Zyklon B was a gas that was used by the Nazis to kill many Jews.

Because of their actions, many other people suffered and died.

Film was often an exception to this impersonal focus. Both Allied and German films vividly showed the human cost. For example, on November 29, the prosecution showed an Allied film of concentration camp liberations. The scenes that had shocked and sickened men like General Eisenhower had the same effect in the courtroom. Many observers were in tears.

The Defense

Long before the trial began, the Allies had decided that "following orders" would be no defense. A chain of command could not relieve individuals of moral responsibility for their own acts. British prosecutor Sir Hartley Shawcross made this point strongly in his opening address to the court:

> ... it is no excuse for the common thief to say, "I stole because I was told to steal," for the murderer to plead, "I killed because I was asked to kill." And these men are in no different position [because] it was nations they sought to rob, and whole peoples which they tried to kill.[6]

In spite of this argument, some defendants used the defense of following orders. These men claimed that their refusal to carry out an order would not have changed anything. It would only have ended their careers and maybe even their lives. Someone else would have carried out the order if they had not.

Wilhelm Keitel claimed to be little more than a glorified "errand boy" for Hitler: ". . . if Hitler ordered it, that was good enough for me," he said. "After all, I was only his office chief. . . . I could only transmit commands from the Führer."[7]

This lowly "office chief" was actually a field marshal, in command of all German armed forces. For him, as for other loyal Nazis, Hitler's word was law. This was more than just a figure of speech. Germans of all ranks and stations owed him their unquestioning obedience.

Hermann Göring tried to defend unquestioning obedience to the Führer. He compared it to a monarchy, in which a king or emperor wields absolute authority: "I am of the opinion that for Germany . . . the Leadership Principle—that is, authority from above downwards and responsibility from below upwards—was the only possibility."[8]

Göring did not deal with the moral responsibility of the individual. The closest he came to it was to admit that "a principle, while thoroughly sound in itself, can lead to extremes."[9]

There were many versions of this theme. Most defendants had "reasons" why someone

The Nuremberg Trials

Hermann Göring had once been Hitler's second-in-command.

else was to blame. When faced with death camps and other atrocities, many claimed that they had not known: "For heaven's sake, do you think I would have supported [Nazi anti-Jewish policy] if I had the slightest idea that it would lead to mass murder?" Hermann Göring asked psychologist G. M. Gilbert. "I assure you we never for a moment had such things in mind. I only thought we would eliminate Jews from positions in big business and government, and that was that."[10]

Telling the Truth

Some defendants seemed to be sorry for their actions. For example, Hans Frank, governor-general of occupied Poland, freely turned over his diaries to the Allies. He said he wanted the truth to come out, regardless of what happened to him or anyone else.

The diaries alone were enough to convict Frank of crimes against humanity. For example, he wrote matter-of-factly about plans to starve people to death: "That we sentence 1,200,000 Jews to die of hunger should be noted only marginally [not emphasized or considered important]."[11] He later wrote in the same diary, "We must annihilate the Jews wherever we find them and wherever it is possible."[12]

The Nuremberg Trials

Baldur von Schirach had been head of the Hitler Youth. Members of the organization were trained to hold the same views of hatred the Nazis held.

Baldur von Schirach, former head of the Hitler Youth, denounced Adolf Hitler and anti-Semitism. He admitted in open court that he had misled Germany's young people: ". . . It was my guilt, which I will have to carry before God and the German nation, that . . . [I] educated the German Youth for a man who committed murders millionfold."[13]

Besides testifying to his own guilt, Von Schirach voluntarily wrote an open letter to the young people of Germany. He confessed that he had led the German youth astray and told them that Adolf Hitler had not been worthy of their loyalty. Then he called upon German youth to renounce Nazism, especially anti-Semitism.

Perhaps the best known of the admissions of guilt was that of Albert Speer. At the end of the war, Speer had risked his life to save Germany from Hitler's "scorched earth" policy. In the process, he had realized the evil of Hitler and the whole Nazi regime.

Still, he knew he was partly responsible for that regime. As minister of armaments and munitions, he had kept the Nazi war machine running. He did it using slave labor of the Jews and other Holocaust victims.

Speer not only accepted responsibility for his own actions, but acknowledged the wider responsibility of all German leaders: "Even in an authoritarian system this collective

The Nuremberg Trials

As the war had closed, Albert Speer had tried to prevent Germany's industry from being damaged by Hitler's destructive orders.

responsibility of the leaders must exist; there can be no attempting to withdraw [from it] after the catastrophe."[14]

The Verdicts

On August 31, 1946, the defendants made their final statements to the court. After that, there was nothing to do but wait while the judges made their decision.

On October 1, the judges read the verdicts in open court. Each defendant was then called individually to hear his sentence.

Eleven of the twenty-one defendants were sentenced to death by hanging. These included Hermann Göring, Field Marshall Wilhelm Keitel, and Hans Frank. Three defendants were acquitted, or found not guilty. The rest received various terms of imprisonment. Albert Speer and Baldur von Schirach each received twenty years. Rudolf Hess was sentenced to life, probably avoiding the death penalty because of his uncertain mental condition.

The death sentences were scheduled to be carried out on October 16. On the night of the fifteenth, Hermann Göring committed suicide in his cell. He used a smuggled capsule of poison to cheat the hangman.

The first International Military Tribunal in history ended in October 1946. However, the

The Nuremberg Trials

Because he fully admitted his guilt, Baldur von Schirach (right) was sentenced by the court to serve twenty years in prison.

Crimes and Criminals of the Holocaust

campaign against war criminals did not end there. The Allies were aggressively seeking and arresting suspects from all walks of life. Plans were already underway for more trials. Considering the horrors of the Holocaust, nothing but an all-out effort would do.

4

"I Was Just Doing My Job"

Many nations that had suffered under Nazi rule conducted their own trials of people who had committed crimes within their borders. The United States, Great Britain, France, and the Soviet Union held trials in the zones they occupied. These "subsequent Nuremberg trials," as they came to be called, targeted the people who carried out the criminal orders of their leaders.

The defense of following orders worked no better for lower-ranked defendants than it did for their superiors. Again and again, courts held that orders could not justify mass murder, medical experiments on helpless prisoners, or the brutalities of slave labor.

The Concentration Camp Trials

Dozens of trials involved staff members of concentration camps and extermination centers. These Nazi staffers were directly responsible for the torture and killing of millions. For example, more than two hundred thousand people died at the Majdanek camp near the Polish city of Lubin. Some were gassed. Others died of disease, exhaustion, or starvation.

Prisoners at Majdanek concentration camp were forced to do back-breaking labor, always with the possibility of being gassed to death hanging over their heads.

"I Was Just Doing My Job"

Majdanek was liberated by the Soviet army on July 24, 1944. The Poles wasted no time dispensing justice. In early 1945, they assembled a special tribunal to judge the case against six members of the senior staff. Two male defendants committed suicide before the end of the trial. The other four received death sentences.

A second Majdanek trial convened in 1946, with ninety-five SS defendants. Most of these men had been guards. Seven were sentenced to death; the rest to long prison terms.

Almost thirty years later, there would be a third Majdanek trial. This one involved sixteen people who had managed to escape detection for all those years. Eight were convicted and one acquitted. Charges against the rest were dropped for reasons such as ill health or unavailability of witnesses.

All three Majdanek trials together only skimmed the surface. A total of 117 Majdanek defendants were held to answer for their crimes. The camp had had a staff of about thirteen hundred. Doubtlessly, many who brutalized and killed prisoners were never held accountable for their actions.

This was true of the camps in general. It was impossible to deal with everyone who mistreated prisoners. The best the Allies could hope for was to bring the worst offenders to justice.

Crimes and Criminals of the Holocaust

The defendants who were found guilty during the first Majdanek trial were executed near the camp's crematoria. It was in that building that they had put many Jews to death during the war years.

The Doctors' Trial

On December 9, 1946, the United States Military Tribunal began the trial of twenty-two Nazi doctors and one medical assistant. They were charged with crimes against humanity for conducting brutal experiments on concentration camp prisoners. These experiments included such things as plunging prisoners into freezing water to see how long they could survive, breaking bones to learn how to set them, and infecting test

"I Was Just Doing My Job"

subjects with diseases such as malaria and tuberculosis to study possible cures.

Many test subjects were left with permanent handicaps because of these experiments. Others died, or were deliberately killed. Dr. Josef Mengele of Auschwitz once murdered fourteen children in a single night so he could perform autopsies, or after-death examinations, on their bodies.

In another cruel experiment, Dr. Wilhelm Beiglboeck of Dachau tested chemicals to

A doctor points out the huge scar on the leg of a Polish survivor during the doctors' trial at Nuremberg.

determine whether they could make seawater safe for drinking. He knew the dangers to his subjects. Drinking salt water long enough and in large enough quantities can kill a human being.

Because of these dangers, Beiglboeck wanted a captive population of "inferior" people for test subjects. He chose forty Gypsies at the Dachau concentration camp.

Karl Hoellenrainer was one of Beiglboeck's subjects. On the witness stand at the Doctors' Trial, he described his experiences:

> At first we got potatoes, milk, and then we got these cookies and . . . rusks [sweetened biscuits]. That lasted about 1 week. Then we got nothing at all. . . . Then the doctor . . . said, 'Now you have to drink sea water on an empty stomach.' . . . We drank two or three times a day. . . . After a few days the people became raving mad; they foamed at the mouth.[1]

At least three people are believed to have died in this experiment. Hoellenrainer saw them carried out on stretchers, with sheets covering their bodies: "We never saw these three again, neither at work nor anywhere in the camp. . . . We thought that they were dead . . ."[2]

For his role in these experiments, Wilhelm Beiglboeck was found guilty of war crimes and crimes against humanity. He was sentenced to fifteen years in prison. In spite of

"I Was Just Doing My Job"

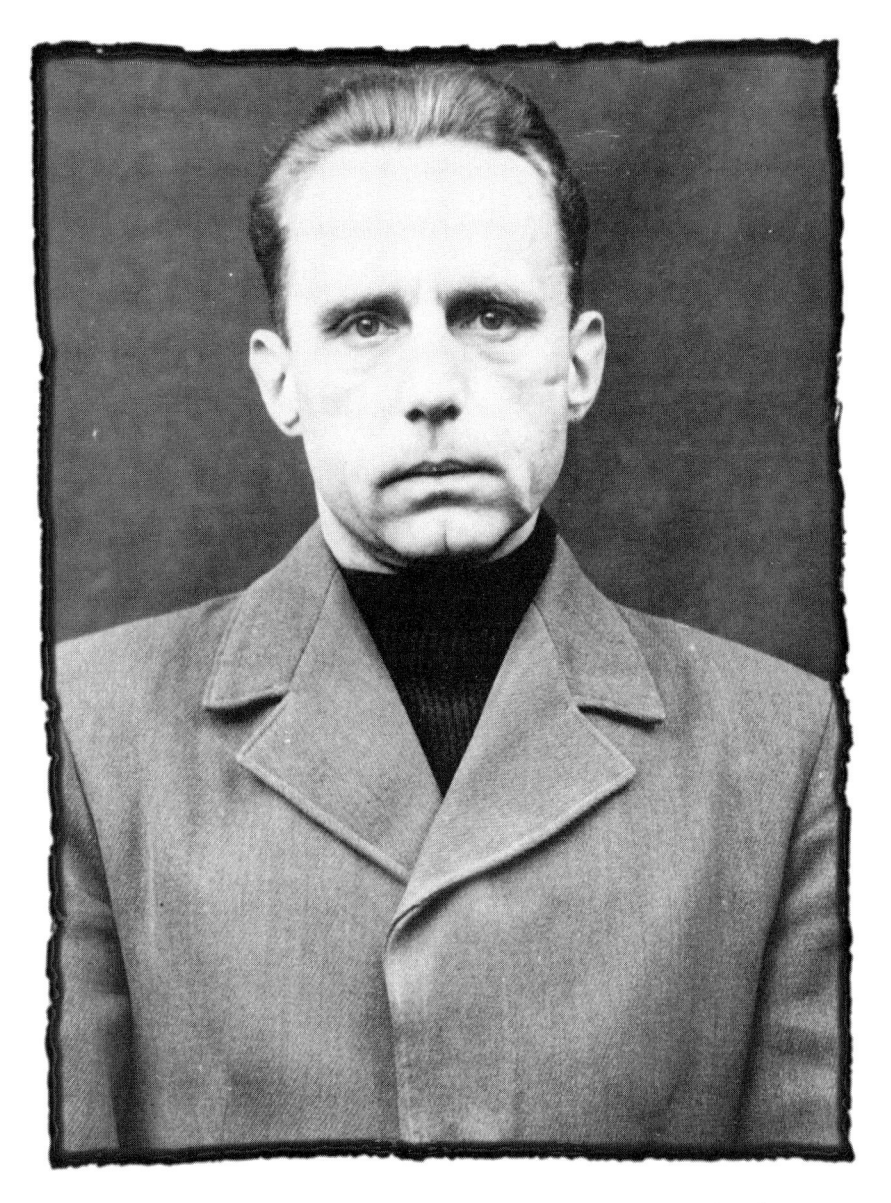

This portrait of Wilhelm Beiglboeck was taken at the time of his trial at Nuremberg.

A notoriously cruel doctor, Joseph Mengele fled to South America and escaped justice.

the powerful case against him, Wilhelm Beiglboeck's sentence was later reduced to ten years on appeal.

Josef Mengele fled to South America in 1949. He assumed a new identity and was never captured. He died in a drowning incident in 1979, but his remains were not identified until 1985.

Of the twenty-three medical professionals placed on trial, nine were sentenced to prison terms of varying lengths. Seven were acquitted and seven were sentenced to death.

The Einsatzgruppen Trial

On September 29, 1947, the United States Military Tribunal began proceedings against twenty-four *Einsatzgruppe* members. The Einsatzgruppen followed the regular army into the Soviet Union. They were death squads; their only job was to kill civilians.

Otto Ohlendorf, commander of one Einsatzgruppe, estimated that his group alone killed ninety thousand children,

"I Was Just Doing My Job"

These Soviet civilians were shot to death by the Einsatzgruppen death squads.

women, and men in one year. Ohlendorf took great pains to explain that the executions were carried out "in a military manner."[3] This means that all the victims were quickly executed by firing squad, without attempts to torture them or prolong their dying.

The reason for this procedure was not pity for the victims. Ohlendorf admitted as much in a sworn statement: "I never sanctioned shootings by individuals. I always gave

Otto Ohlendorf testifies during his trial. He received a death sentence.

orders for several people to shoot [together], in order to avoid any individual having to take direct, personal responsibility."[4]

Ohlendorf's attempt to portray himself as an honest soldier forced to do a disagreeable job did not impress the tribunal. He was sentenced to death and hanged at Landsberg Prison in 1951.

Thirteen other defendants were also sentenced to death, though the sentence was later reduced for ten of them. Of the other defendants, one committed suicide and another was judged too ill to stand trial. One was sentenced to time served and released. The rest received prison terms ranging from ten years to life.

The Stroop Trial

In 1951, SS General Jürgen Stroop was serving a life term in prison for crimes committed against American prisoners of war. A Polish court asked the United States to extradite him so he could be tried for the destruction of the Warsaw ghetto in 1943. The Americans complied.

Stroop's 1947 American trial had lasted more than three weeks. His 1951 Polish trial lasted only six days. Part of the reason for this was Stroop's own written record of his activities in Warsaw.

Crimes and Criminals of the Holocaust

In a report to his superiors in Berlin, Stroop stated:

> [I] decided to destroy the entire Jewish residential area by setting every block on fire. . . . [Sometimes] Jews . . . [jumped] down from the upper stories . . . into the street from the burning buildings. With their bones broken, they still tried to crawl across the street into blocks of buildings which had not yet been set on fire. . . .[5]

On May 24, 1943, Stroop summed up the destruction of the ghetto with facts and figures. He stated that 56,065 Jews were caught, and 13,929 of that number

Jürgen Stroop (second from left in foreground) watches buildings burn in the Warsaw ghettos. He had ordered his troops to set the buildings on fire in order to end the ghetto uprising.

"destroyed" (killed). He also estimated that a further "5,000 to 6,000 Jews were destroyed by being blown up or by perishing in the flames."[6]

On the strength of his own words, Jürgen Stroop was sentenced to death by hanging. The sentence was carried out on September 8, 1951, on the site of the Warsaw ghetto.

The Limits of Individual Responsibility

Not all war criminals were killers or the commanders of killers. In deciding who to prosecute, the various war crimes courts questioned the limits of personal responsibility. Were judges who handed out death sentences for minor offenses guilty of crimes? Were industrialists, who used slave labor to manufacture weapons and other war materials? What about the men whose company kept the death camps supplied with Zyklon B poison gas?

Judges, factory operators, and chemical suppliers were indeed found guilty of serious crimes. For example, Judge Oswald Rothaug used the law as a weapon against Jews, Poles, and other "subhumans." In one famous case, he sentenced a Jewish businessman to death for allowing a German woman to sit on his lap. On December 4, 1947, Oswald Rothaug was sentenced to life in prison by a United States military court.

Officers of two large German companies, the Krupp Works and I. G. Farben, were convicted of several crimes, including the use of slave labor. Krupp operated iron and steel works along with mining operations. The company also manufactured armaments. I. G. Farben was the chemical company that manufactured the Zyklon B gas used in the death camps, along with products such as synthetic rubber, explosives, and gunpowder.

Both companies used thousands of slave laborers. Their officers knew that these people

Prisoners from Auschwitz concentration camp were forced to build the Krupp factory.

would literally be worked to death. The workers were kept on starvation rations in disease-infested barracks, working ten to twelve hours daily. Few workers lived longer than three to six months under these conditions.

For crimes that included allowing this inhuman treatment, eleven executives from Krupp and thirteen from I. G. Farben were convicted in two separate trials. Their prison terms ranged from one to twelve years.

One of the most stunning of the later trial verdicts occurred in the British Occupation Zone. Dr. Bruno Tesch and two of his employees in the firm of Tesch and Stabenow stood trial for supplying Zyklon B to the death camps. The company was not involved in manufacture. It distributed the gas under a license from the I. G. Farben division that actually produced it.

One employee, technician Joachim Drosihn, was found not guilty because he had no control over the gas supply. Tesch and his chief clerk, Karl Weinbacher, not only controlled the supply, but sold Zyklon B in full knowledge that it was being used to kill human beings. For this crime, both men were sentenced to death.

Lessons in Accountability

The postwar trials exposed and punished Nazi atrocities. In the process, they paved the way for a truly international response to mass murder and terrorism. The world looked at what the Nazis did and said *No*. This should never happen again.

People could not escape blame for their actions because they were "just following orders," or even because they never personally killed or brutalized anyone. Even in war there are limits. Those who cross the line can—and should—be punished.

5

Fugitives From Justice

Many Holocaust survivors had a difficult time readjusting to normal life. Some wanted only to forget—to put the past behind them and quiet the nightmares that ruined their sleep. Others, like Nazi hunter Simon Wiesenthal, wanted to remember.

Wiesenthal spent the war years in several different concentration camps. Many times he escaped death by a stroke of luck. To him, memory is the price he pays for surviving while so many others died: "I am asking myself what I can do for those who have not survived. [My answer] is: I want to be their mouthpiece, I want to keep their memory alive, to make sure the dead live on in that memory."[1]

Nazi hunting was Wiesenthal's way of

Crimes and Criminals of the Holocaust

Simon Wiesenthal became a leading Nazi hunter and Holocaust activist.

remembering the dead and finding some measure of justice for the living. Others who shared these goals include Serge and Beate Klarsfeld and Israeli security agent Isser Harel.

The Nazi hunters have tracked fugitives all over the world, bringing many to justice. Their cases have included people at all levels of the Nazi death machine, from Adolf Eichmann, who coordinated the whole extermination program, to camp commandants and brutal guards.

The Case of Adolf Eichmann

Adolf Eichmann did not look or act like a mass murderer. The man who became the object of one of the biggest manhunts in history seemed entirely ordinary, even drab. He never killed anyone with his own hands or tortured helpless prisoners.

At the height of his career, he was little more than a clerk. He kept records. He ordered supplies. He juggled train schedules.

Eichmann did these things in Berlin, and somewhere else, people died. Somewhere else, Jews would be crammed into boxcars and taken to death camps. Eichmann was a "desk murderer." He ran the massive extermination program as if it were a business—and he did it with deadly efficiency.

After the war, neither the Allies nor the Nazi hunters fully understood Eichmann's importance. By the time they realized that he was the man who had kept the Nazi extermination machine running, he had slipped away.

For fifteen years, Adolf Eichmann was the subject of one of the largest manhunts in history. Simon Wiesenthal tracked him relentlessly. So did the government of the new state of Israel. In 1960, he was found living as "Ricardo Klement" in Buenos Aires, Argentina.

However, the Israelis knew that the Argentine government would refuse to turn Eichmann over to them. Therefore, they decided to kidnap him. Isser Harel, head of the Israeli intelligence agency *Mossad*, took personal charge of the operation.

In May 1960, the Israelis grabbed "Ricardo Klement" off the street and smuggled him out of the country. Eleven months later, on April 10, 1961, the trial of Adolf Eichmann began.

Throughout the trial, Eichmann claimed he was innocent of war crimes because he was just following orders. The Israeli prosecutors carefully documented every charge. They showed Eichmann's guilt, and the precision with which the killing operation was organized and carried out.

Fugitives From Justice

Adolf Eichmann takes notes during his trial. The booth he sat in was made of bulletproof glass.

In December 1961, Eichmann was found guilty and sentenced to death. He was executed on June 1, 1962, at midnight.

The Case of Franz Stangl

Franz Stangl served as commandant of two extermination camps, Sobibór and then Treblinka. In less than eighteen months at these two camps, he supervised the murder of more than ninety thousand men, women, and children.

Stangl kept his distance from the actual killing, but he would come to the unloading platform, dressed in "white linen riding clothes and [cracking] his whip like a horseman."[2] He would watch as the prisoners were herded off the trains and into "the tube"—a corridor of barbed-wire fencing that led to the gas chambers.

A survivor from Sobibór noted that Stangl "seemed oddly out of place, almost as if he had interrupted his dinner to greet the Jews and was eager to get back to it before it turned cold."[3]

After the war, Stangl was taken into custody because of his work in the euthanasia (mercy killing) program. Under this program, almost three hundred thousand physically and mentally handicapped people were killed by the Nazis. He managed to hide his

Fugitives From Justice

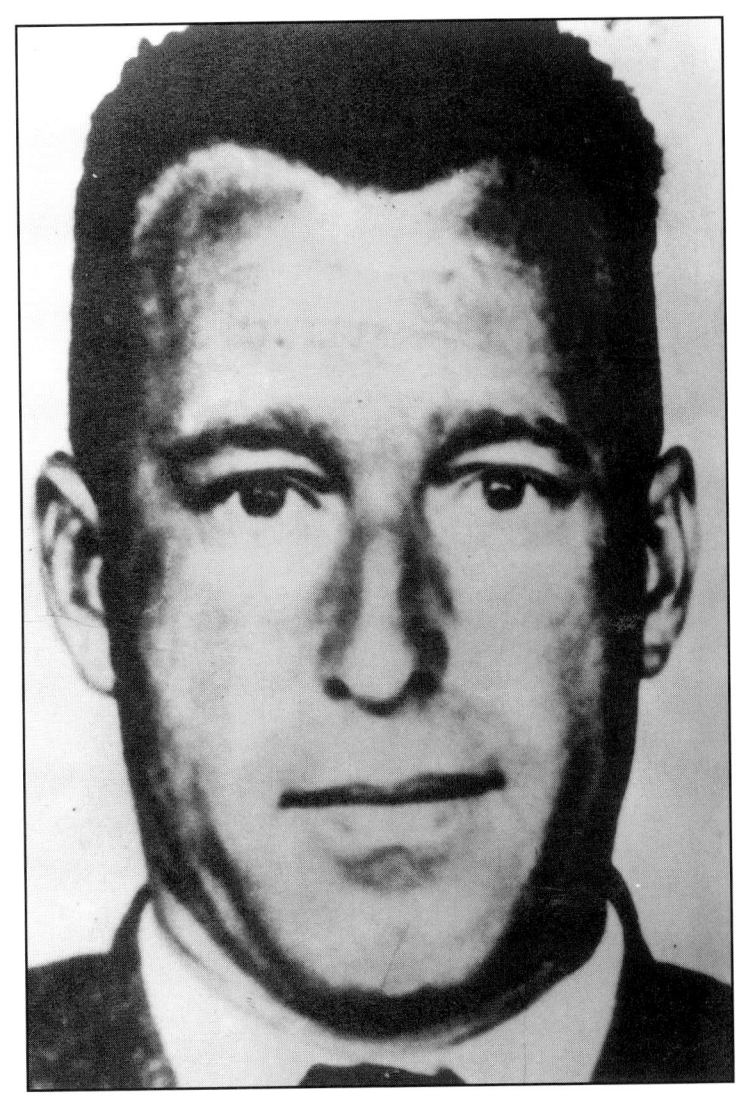

Franz Stangl oversaw the murders of tens of thousands of people at Nazi extermination camps.

role at Sobibór and Treblinka. Later, he escaped from custody and fled to Italy, then to Syria. In 1951, Stangl and his whole family got visas, or travel permits, to go to Brazil. They would live there peacefully for many years.

By 1964, Simon Wiesenthal had uncovered Stangl's record at Sobibór and Treblinka. So had the Austrian government. Because Stangl was Austrian by birth, the government issued a warrant (legal order) for his arrest.

Wiesenthal found Stangl through an informant. After locating him, Wiesenthal proceeded with great caution. If Stangl was warned, he could disappear before the authorities had a chance to arrest him. Wiesenthal sent the warrant and request for extradition to a trusted source: the Austrian ambassador to Brazil.

On February 28, 1967, Franz Stangl was arrested on his way home from work. In addition to the Austrian warrant, both West Germany and Poland requested the extradition, or legal transfer, of Stangl. After more than three months of legal wrangling, the Brazilian Supreme Court ruled that Franz Stangl should be extradited to West Germany.

The trial did not begin until May 13, 1970, and it lasted for more than seven months. When it ended, Franz Stangl was found guilty of crimes against humanity and sentenced to life in prison. As it turned out, his life lasted only six months. Stangl died of heart failure on June 28, 1971.

"That is enough for a life sentence," said Wiesenthal. "The important thing is that he was brought to trial. The spirit of the law is that everyone who is killed has the right to a trial of his killers."[4]

The Case of Hermine Braunsteiner

Another case that captured Simon Wiesenthal's attention was that of Hermine Braunsteiner. She had been a brutal guard in the women's barracks at the Majdanek concentration camp. Perhaps her crimes were not as extensive as Eichmann's, but she was particularly vicious and sadistic. She enjoyed inflicting pain.

Survivors told Wiesenthal that Braunsteiner

> used a vicious dog and a whip weighted with lead.... She enjoyed flogging us, she enjoyed it when we screamed and even more when we fainted.... When mothers with children were brought to the camp, she'd tear the children away.[5]

Because Braunsteiner was Austrian by birth, Wiesenthal did not have to travel far from his Vienna headquarters to track down her relatives. He sent a young German who

Crimes and Criminals of the Holocaust

Hermine Braunsteiner thought she had escaped justice, until Simon Wiesenthal caught up with her.

could gain the confidence of the family to talk with them.

The agent was able to discover that Braunsteiner had gone to Canada and later married an American. Her married name, the relatives said, was Ryan. With this much information, the rest was easy.

Through contacts in Canada, Wiesenthal tracked the former guard to Queens, New York, where she was living quietly as the wife of Russell Ryan. According to her shocked neighbors, Hermine Ryan was "a quiet person who never bothers anybody."[6] She was pleasant, fond of children, and well-liked in the community. Many considered this proof that Hermine Ryan could not possibly have been the monstrous Hermine Braunsteiner.

Simon Wiesenthal knew better:

> [many of] my "clients" were . . . solid family men and women, devoted to their children, loyal to their relatives. . . . good citizens and good neighbours who did their duty, tended their gardens, and seldom made trouble for anyone.[7]

This was one of the most frightening truths of the Holocaust: Ordinary people could turn into "monsters" and back again. That said something about human nature that many people did not want to believe.

In 1973, Hermine Braunsteiner-Ryan was extradited from the United States to West

Germany. On November 26, 1975, she became one of the sixteen defendants in the third and last Majdanek trial.

The trial was the longest war-crimes proceeding in West German history. It lasted more than five-and-a-half years. When it was over, Hermine Braunsteiner Ryan found herself facing two life terms. By imposing this double sentence, the court blocked any chance that she might one day win her freedom.

The Case of Klaus Barbie

In 1942, the city of Lyons, France, was a center of the French Resistance. Jews and others who had run afoul of the Nazis found refuge in the city. In November, the Gestapo sent a young officer named Klaus Barbie to get the situation under control.

They chose Barbie because he would not hesitate to torture or kill as many people as necessary. In Lyons, Barbie soon proved to be as murderous as his superiors had believed; people called him the Butcher of Lyons. "He was savage. . . . It was unimaginable," said survivor Ennat Leger. "He broke my teeth. . . . He put a bottle in my mouth and pushed it until the lips split from the pressure."[8]

During his time in Lyons, Barbie tracked down forty-four Jewish children hidden in the village of Izieu and sent them to Auschwitz.

Fugitives From Justice

Serge Klarsfeld (pictured) helped get Klaus Barbie sent to France so he could stand trial for his crimes.

Crimes and Criminals of the Holocaust

When he caught and killed resistance leader Jean Moulin, he received a medal. Hitler himself presented it.

After the war, Klaus Barbie managed to escape arrest. By 1951, he had made his way to South America. Twenty years later, Nazi hunters Serge and Beate Klarsfeld found him in Bolivia, living under the name Klaus Altmann.

It took the Klarsfelds twelve years to convince the Bolivian government to extradite Barbie to France. In 1983, the Butcher returned to Lyons as a prisoner of the French government. At his trial, survivors joined relatives of Barbie's victims to testify against him. On July 4, 1987, a French jury sentenced the Butcher of Lyons to life in prison. At the time of that sentence, Barbie's crimes were more than forty years old. Barbie himself was seventy-three.

History and Memory

On July 22, 1997, ten years after Barbie was sentenced, eighty-four-year-old Erich Priebke was convicted of the 1944 execution of 335 Italian civilians. He killed them under orders, in retaliation for an attack on German occupation troops. The world press heralded this as quite probably the last war crimes trial from World War II.

Fugitives From Justice

Klaus Barbie's reign of terror occurred in Lyons, France, where more than forty years later, he returned in handcuffs in 1983.

Crimes and Criminals of the Holocaust

From the beginning of the International Tribunal on October 18, 1945, to the end of the Priebke appeals trial on March 7, 1998, more than half a century had passed. Victims have been mourned, refugees resettled, at least some perpetrators brought to justice. Survivors have learned to live with the horrors of their past.

Soon the Holocaust will pass out of living memory; no one will be left to tell the story first hand. Survivors and others are trying to make sure it never passes out of historical memory. They tell their stories, they create memorials, they set up foundations for studying the Holocaust. They do these things to give meaning to their own lives and to pass the torch of memory to new generations.

Timeline

July 24, 1944—Soviet army liberates Majdanek death camp.

January 27, 1945—Soviet army liberates Auschwitz.

March 19, 1945—Hitler issues his scorched earth order.

April 11, 1945—U.S. Army liberates Buchenwald concentration camp.

April 21, 1945—Soviet forces reach Berlin.

April 29, 1945—Adolf Hitler marries Eva Braun.

April 30, 1945—Hitler and his new wife committ suicide.

May 7, 1945—Germany surrenders unconditionally to the Allies.

June 26, 1945—United Nations Charter approved.

September 1945—Harrison Commission issues its report on conditions in DP camps.

October 18, 1945—Nazi leaders are indicted by the International Military Tribunal.

October 24, 1945—United Nations Charter goes into effect.

November 20, 1945—First public session of the Nuremberg trials begins.

Crimes and Criminals of the Holocaust

August 31, 1946—Albert Speer makes his final statement to the International Tribunal.

October 1, 1946—Nuremberg verdicts are read in open court.

October 15, 1946—Hermann Göring commits suicide in his cell.

October 16, 1946—Nuremberg defendants who were sentenced to death are hanged.

December 9, 1946—The United States Military Tribunal begins the Doctors' Trial.

September 29, 1947—United States Military Tribunal begins the Einsatzgruppen Trial.

November 29, 1947—State of Israel created by the United Nations General Assembly.

September 1951—Jürgen Stroop is hanged for destruction of the Warsaw ghetto in 1943.

May 1960—Israeli agents kidnap Adolf Eichmann.

April 10, 1961—The trial of Adolf Eichmann begins in Israel.

December 15, 1961—Eichmann is found guilty and sentenced to death.

June 1, 1962—Eichmann is executed.

February 28, 1967—Franz Stangl is arrested.

May 13, 1970—The trial of Franz Stangl begins.

December 22, 1970—Stangl is sentenced to life in prison.

Timeline

June 28, 1971—Stangl dies of heart failure in prison.

July 4, 1987—Klaus Barbie is sentenced to life in prison.

May 8, 1996—The first trial of Erich Priebke begins.

March 7, 1998—Priebke is found guilty at his second trial.

Chapter Notes

Chapter 1. A Time of Reckoning

1. Michael R. Marrus, *The Nuremberg War Crimes Trial 1945–46: A Documentary History* (Boston: Bedford/St. Martin's, 1997), p. 25.

2. General Vassily Petrenko, Interviewed by Sanchia Berg, "Today Programme," *BBC Radio 4*, January 25, 2001 <http://www.bbc.co.uk/history/war/wwtwo/holocaust/general_petrenko_1.shtml> (January 29, 2002).

3. Ian Kershaw, *Hitler 1936–1945: Nemesis* (New York: W. W. Norton & Co., 2000), p. 757.

4. Ibid., p. 751.

5. Michael Burleigh, *The Third Reich: A New History* (New York: Hill and Wang, 2000), p. 790.

6. Cornelius Ryan, *The Last Battle* (New York: Simon & Schuster, 1995), p. 172.

7. Ibid., p. 348.

8. Ibid., p. 409.

9. Burleigh, p. 793.

Chapter 2. The Victims

1. Jacob Biber, *Risen From the Ashes* (San Bernardino, Calif.: The Borgo Press, 1990), p. 11.

2. Ibid.

Chapter Notes

3. Anton Gill, *The Journey Back From Hell: An Oral History—Conversations With Concentration Camp Survivors* (New York: William Morrow and Company, Inc., 1988), p. 40.

4. Ibid., pp. 39–40.

5. "The Displaced Person," *GTEL® Georgia Tech Electronic Library.* n.d. <https://www.library.getech.edu/projects/holocaust/person.htm> (May 30, 2003).

6. Walter Laqueur, ed., *The Holocaust Encyclopedia* (New Haven, Conn.: Yale University Press, 2001), pp. 152, 154.

7. Hella Pick, *Simon Wiesenthal: A Life in Search of Justice* (Boston: Northeastern University Press, 1996), p. 83.

8. Laqueur, p. 154.

9. Isabella Leitner with Irving A. Leitner, *Saving the Fragments: From Auschwitz to New York* (New York: New American Library, 1985), p. 54.

10. Howard M. Sachar, *A History of Israel From the Rise of Zionism to Our Time,* second edition (New York: Alfred A. Knopf, 1996), p. 256.

11. Ibid.

Chapter 3. The Nuremberg Trials

1. Michael R. Marrus, *The Nuremberg War Crimes Trial 1945–46: A Documentary History* (Boston: Bedford/St Martin's, 1997), p. 58.

2. Ibid., p. 70.

3. Justice Jackson's Opening Statement for the Prosecution, "Second Day, Wednesday, 11/21/1945, Part 04," *Trial of the Major War Criminals before the International Military Tribunal, Volume II,* Proceedings: 11/14/1945–11/30/1945, Nuremberg: IMT, 1947, pp. 98–102 <http://www.law.umkc.edu/faculty/projects/ftrials/nuremberg/Jackson.html> (February 18, 2002).

4. Ibid.

5. Ibid.

6. Marrus, p. 88.

7. G. M. Gilbert, *Nuremberg Diary* (New York: Farrar, Straus and Company, 1947), p. 108.

8. Marrus, p. 105.

9. Ibid.

10. Gilbert, p. 208.

11. Ibid., pp. 68–69.

12. Ibid., p. 71.

13. Ibid., p. 349.

14. Albert Speer, *Inside the Third Reich* (New York: Macmillan, 1970), p. 516.

Chapter 4. "I Was Just Doing My Job"

1. Kevin Mahoney, ed., *In Pursuit of Justice: Examining the Evidence of the Holocaust* (Washington, D.C.: United States Holocaust Memorial Council, n.d.), p. 97.

2. Ibid.

3. Ibid., p. 158.

4. Ernst Klee, Willi Dressen, and Volker Riess, eds., *The Good Old Days*, trans. Deborah Burnstone (New York: Konecky & Konecky, 1991), p. 60.

5. Nazi Conspiracy and Aggression, Volume 1, "The Stroop Report," Chapter VII (Washington D.C.: United Stated Government Printing Office, 1946), pp. 995–998 <http://fcit.coedu.usf.edu/holocaust/resource/document/DocStroo.htm> (April 22, 2002).

6. Ibid.

Chapter 5. Fugitives From Justice

1. Simon Wiesenthal, *Justice Not Vengeance* (New York: Grove-Weidenfeld, 1989), p. 351.

2. Alan Levy, *The Wiesenthal File* (Grand Rapids, Mich.: William B. Eerdmans Publishing Company, 1993), p. 279.

3. Ibid.

4. Ibid., pp. 316–317.

5. Ibid., p. 322.

6. Ibid., p. 325.

7. Ibid.

8. Jewish Virtual Library, "Klaus Barbie," 2002 <http://www.us-israel.org/jsource/Holocaust/Barbie.html> (April 25, 2002).

Glossary

accused—To be formally charged with wrongdoing.

Allies—The nations joined in the war against Germany and its allies, led by Great Britain, the United States, and the Soviet Union.

Axis—The name given to Germany and its allies in World War II.

charge—A claim of wrongdoing made before a court of law.

collaborators—Citizens who cooperate with the army that has occupied their country.

concentration camp—Prison camps where people thought to be enemies of the Nazis were held for prolonged periods. Marked by brutal treatment and the use of prisoners as slave laborers.

convict—To find, or prove, someone guilty of a crime.

death camp—Camps established for the purpose of killing large numbers of people. Often called "death factories."

deportation—Forced relocation of Jews and others.

Glossary

Einsatzgruppen—The killing squads that followed the German army into Soviet territory. Their job was to execute Jews and other "undesirables."

Final Solution—The term applied to Nazi plans to exterminate the Jewish people.

Führer—The title of Adolph Hitler. It literally means "leader."

Führer bunker—An underground bomb shelter where Adolf Hitler and his staff spent the last days of the war.

genocide—The systematic extermination, or attempted extermination, of an entire racial, ethnic, political, or religious group.

Gestapo—*(Geheime-Staats-Polizei)* A secret state police agency in Nazi Germany.

Holocaust—Originally, an all-consuming fire. The term is now also used to describe the extermination of more than 11 million people, including 6 million Jews.

indict—To make a formal accusation of a crime.

international tribunal—A court made up of representatives from many different nations.

propaganda—A presentation of ideas slanted to shape and control public opinion.

Crimes and Criminals of the Holocaust

scorched-earth policy—The policy of laying waste to all land and buildings so nothing will be left for an advancing enemy.

selection—Process of separating prisoners into two groups: those to be killed immediately and those to be used for slave labor.

SS *(Shutzstaffel)* **"protection squad"**—The elite guard of the Nazi state. It administered the Final Solution and insured obedience to the dictates of the Führer.

slave labor—Jews and others forced to work for the Nazis. Thousands of them were starved and worked literally to death.

Zionism—An organized movement to build a Jewish state in Palestine.

Zyklon B—The commercial name of the poison gas used in the gas chambers at Auschwitz-Birkenau and other killing centers.

Further Reading

Anderson, Christopher J., and John P. Langellier. *The Fall of Fortress Europe: From the Battle of the Bulge to the Crossing of the Rhine.* Broomall, Pa.: Chelsea House Publishers, 2001.

Black, Wallace B., and Jean F. Blashfield. *Victory in Europe.* Parsippany, N.J.: Crestwood House, 1993.

Giblin, James Cross. *The Life and Death of Adolf Hitler.* New York: Clarion Books, 2002.

Rice, Jr., Earl. *The Nuremberg Trials.* Farmington Hills, Mich.: Gale Group, 1996.

Samuel, Wolfgang W. E., and Stephen E. Ambrose. *German Boy: A Child in War.* New York: Broadway Books, 2001.

Silverman, Maida. *Israel: The Founding of a Modern Nation.* New York: Dial Books for Young Readers, 1998.

Internet Addresses

Famous World Trials: Nuremberg Trials, 1954–1949.
http://www.law.umkc.edu/faculty/projects/ftrials/nuremberg/nuremberg.htm

Other War Crimes Trials. ©1997.
http://motlc.wiesenthal.org/pages/t004/t00403.html

The Trial of Adolf Eichmann.
http://www.pbs.org/eichmann/

Index

A
American Jewish Joint Distribution Committee, 32
Attlee, Clement, 34
Auschwitz, 13, 86

B
Barbie, Klaus, 86, 88
Beiglboeck, Wilhelm, 63–64
Bormann, Martin, 41
Braun, Eva, 22
Braunsteiner, Hermine, 83, 85

C
Camp Föhrenwald, 26–27, 39
concentration camps, 12, 23, 24, 29, 48, 60–61, 83, 86
conspiracy indictment, 42
crimes against humanity indictment, 42, 43
crimes against peace indictment, 42

D
Dachau, 63
displaced persons (DP) camps, 25, 28, 29, 32
The Doctors' Trial, 62–64, 66

E
Eichmann, Adolf, 77–78, 80
Einsatzgruppen trial, 66, 68–69
Eisenhower, Dwight D., 28–29
euthanasia program, 80
Exodus 1947, 35–36

F
Frank, Hans, 52, 56
French Resistance, 86, 88
Führer bunker, 18, 22

G
Gentile prisoners, 31
Gestapo, 23, 86
Gilbert, G. M., 52
Goebbels, Joseph, 40
Göring, Hermann, 50, 52, 56
Guderian, Heinz, 16

H
Harel, Isser, 77–78
Harrison, Earl G., 28–29
Hess, Rudolf, 41
Himmler, Heinrich, 40
Hitler Youth, 20, 54
Hoellenrainer, Karl, 64
Hofsbach, Friedrich, 15

I
I. G. Farben, 72–73
Israel, 35, 38

J
Jackson, Robert H., 45–46, 48

K
Keitel, Wilhelm, 42, 50, 56
Klarsfeld, Beate, 77, 88
Klarsfeld, Serge, 77, 88
Krupp Works, 72–73

L
Lawrence, Geoffrey, 43
Leadership Principle, 50
Leitner, Isabella, 31
Lyons, France, 86, 88

Crimes and Criminals of the Holocaust

M
Majdanek, 24, 60–61, 83, 86
Mauthausen, 29
Mossad, 78
Moulin, Jean, 88

N
Nazi hunters, 77
Nuremberg trials, 42, 45–46, 48–50, 52, 54, 56, 58, 59

O
Oder River, 19
Ohlendorf, Otto, 66, 68, 69

P
Palace of Justice, 42
Palestine, 33–35, 38
Patton, George S., 28
Petrenko, Vassily, 13
Priebke, Erich, 88

R
refugee, 25
Rentzschmule DP center, 29
Rothaug, Oswald, 71

S
Schirach, Baldur von, 54, 56
scorched-earth policy, 18–20
Shawcross, Hartley, 49
Sobibór, 80
Soviet Army, 13
Speer, Albert, 18, 20, 54, 56
Stangl, Franz, 80
Stroop, Jürgen, 69–71

T
Tesch, Bruno, 73
Treblinka, 80, 82
Truman, Harry S, 28, 29, 34

U
United Nations, 23, 26, 35–36

W
war crimes indictment, 23, 42, 43
Wiesenthal, Simon, 29, 75, 78, 82, 83
Wilson, Francesca, 27

Y
Yishuv, 34

Z
Zionists, 33